T0063198

Experimental Youth Ministry
version 1.0

B.C. Levasseur

WESTBOW
PRESS
A DIVISION OF THOMAS NELSON

Copyright © 2013 B.C. Levasseur.

All rights reserved. No part of this book may be used
or reproduced by any means, graphic, electronic, or
mechanical, including photocopying, recording, taping or
by any information storage retrieval system without the
written permission of the publisher except in the case of
brief quotations embodied in critical articles and reviews.

WestBow Press books may be ordered
through booksellers or by contacting:

WestBow Press
A Division of Thomas Nelson
1663 Liberty Drive
Bloomington, IN 47403
www.westbowpress.com
1 (866) 928-1240

Because of the dynamic nature of the Internet, any web
addresses or links contained in this book may have changed
since publication and may no longer be valid. The views
expressed in this work are solely those of the author and
do not necessarily reflect the views of the publisher, and
the publisher hereby disclaims any responsibility for them.

ISBN: 978-1-4908-1111-6 (sc)
ISBN: 978-1-4908-1112-3 (e)

Library of Congress Control Number: 2013918403

Printed in the United States of America.

WestBow Press rev. date: 12/18/2013

Thanks to
James & April Cogdill
And
Mrs. Emily A. Duda, MDiv.

For your examples gave me courage
and encouragement to write my
first book and to finish it.

Table of Contents

Dedication 9
Author's Notes and Instructions 11
Preface 15
Introductions 19
    Subjects 21
    Salvation 25
    Μαρτυρέω 28
    Prayer 30
    Mystery 33
    Claim 36
    Integrate 40
    Rites 43
    Recycle 46
    Many Mind 49
    Passion 52
    Ingenuity 54
    Teach 57
    Disciple 60
    Danger 64
    Mission 67
Final Notes and Challenges 72
Material, Subjects, and People
Worth Referencing 79

Dedication

This is to all those who seek truth without a traditional guide, who seek justice without approved scales, who seek wisdom without a standard compass. This is to those with ears to hear what the Spirit says to the Churches; for the only way is Christ.

This is to those who have sought for salvation among men, who search for the Divine among mortals, who cannot see or understand the deformities and perversions we have brought upon ourselves; for the only truth is Christ.

This is to all the people who have been damaged by failure, injured by human inability, haunted by hesitation -casualties of the unspoken war waged by hypocrisy and legalism; for the only life is Christ.

This is to all those people out there who —for the sake of freedom, increased intimacy with YHWH, advancing the Kingdom of Heaven while reducing the size of

Christendom— have joined in the sufferings of our LORD at the hands of HIS bride, the Church; for Christ is.

Dedication

1. Matthew 22

Author's Notes and Instructions

It took a long time to write this small book. At first, it was just a collection of rants —essays of whatever brought my blood to boil about a host of subjects. I read what I had created and hated it; it sounded angry, cynical, negative, hopeless, and derelict of merit and use.

I started again. This time I argued with myself which added some counterpoint; however, the trouble is that when you argue with yourself, you always win — except you don't.

When I attempted to add a third voice, I thought, "Who would want to read

Interact Here

This space is left intentionally blank for you the reader; for your thoughts, notes, and ideas.

about me arguing with myself and I?"

That is when I began to detach the Three Characters from myself —just remove myself from the equation— and give them viewpoints of their own: three opposites. I stopped trying to instill my own ideas and tried to focus on what the reader might want: a way for you to find your own ideas. It would be impossible to write a youth ministry book that could encompass every situation, every context.

I decided to make a book that might help the reader with their own search. This requires a bit of participation of the reader and no small amount of homework. I write vaguely with intention. Large margins are provided for

note taking. Don't just read; **Interact Here**
interact.

I wish there were an
easier way.

Preface

Three ministers of youth found themselves in a shelter underneath the earth while the government or other militants caused chaos above, or perhaps it was a natural disaster; that minor detail was lost, and the timeline of the goings-on outside coincides with either. The point is that these Three found themselves sealed off from the outside world for an extended period of time. The events which caused this gathering matter little.

Care will be taken that only the most important details of this encounter shall be preserved: the words they exchanged. While the times in prayer, pauses for thought, surplus of emotions expressed, tense moments of silence, doctrinal or personally identifying information given and observed, or means of survival and hygiene used during this time of trouble did occur —they have not been preserved. Only their words have been recorded so that the rest of us may consider them without such unnecessary burdens influencing our thoughts, feelings, or conclusions —for that is the purpose. Some such references will be provided for the extracurricular.

Everything recorded is intended to provoke thought. An idea that is challenged may stand or fall; new ideas may replace the fallen; older ways may be proven strong once again. Many things were discussed; each subject —each line— may stand alone, or they may not.

These Three ministers spoke as some who assumed their audience to be GOD-fearing, thinking ones who strive to live and to be what they have read in the Sacred Words, and who are never content towards comfort. Their status as ordained or lay ministers will not be defined, but those Three did hold the things they discussed quite dearly. They observed and expressed themselves in three distinct manners. It was their wish that their last moments be used to the greatest effect for HIS Kingdom and glory and for the strengthening and edification of HIS Church —not our Church. Take your time, think, ponder, contemplate, meditate, pray; they did.

Preface

1. Plato
2. Aristotle
3. Eusibius
4. George Orwell

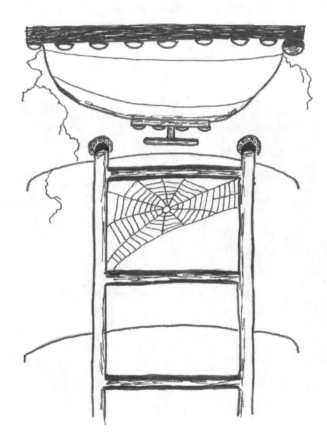

Introductions

These are the names of the Three ministers of youth who were gathered in this place according to HIS perfect will along with the words they used to describe themselves in Latin and Greek:

Canon Q. McKinsey: formalis instabilitas; κανονικος κίνηση

Filip Mann: filius maneo; τέκνον χρόνιος

Eudokia "Doc" Adams: affectus adamans; ευδοκια άδαμας

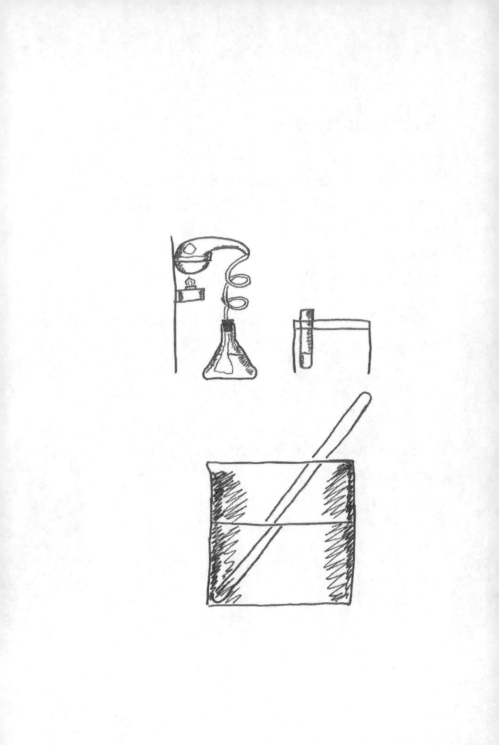

Variable: Subjects

With no youths, to whom shall I minister?

Are you wondering about our purpose now that they are gone?

Have you heard the one about the pastor who was stranded -alone- one a desert island?

No, I have not.

Neither have I. What is a minister when the minister is the only one left?

If HE is our Shepherd, then what is a pastor in *HIS* pasture?

A disciple is still a disciple -even when the disciple has no disciples.

I would rather we not be stranded on an island nor secluded in a monastery.

There are benefits to retreats.

We are not on a retreat.

Why not?

Retreats are not permanent. How would such a thing benefit the community of Christians at large?

There are tales of Christians who, long ago, would live their whole lives in seclusion. They were considered great among our people.

Wasn't that a rare occurrence?

Does rarity negate value?

Was it not also a choice, usually? Our seclusion is one of necessity. Normally, the rest of us must work in the Community.

Long ago, the priests were given a task: to minister before the LORD. A secluded minister still has an audience.

To what avail? What good is it to preach to a choir?

What would such a thing look like?

Have you ever rehearsed a sermon by yourself? Have you ever imagined HIM in one of your pews or sitting in on one of your meetings? We are the subjects and HE is our King.

Are ministers sheep, too?

To be leaders in a community dedicated to following someone other than ourselves . . . ?

What does this change?

In this, I sense apprehension as though a great expectation

Interact Here was focused on all with whom I interact.

How might one go about ministry as though GOD were micromanaging every detail, and then how do I go about ministry as though HE does not?

Variable: Subjects

1. John 10
2. Matthew 28
3. John 13
4. 1–2Timothy
5. 1 Peter 5
6. Ephesians 3, 4
7. Titus 1
8. Ignatius of Loyola
9. Antony of Egypt
10. 1 Chronicles 15

Variable: Salvation

Interact Here

Have all those to whom you minister been saved?

Empirical evidence is very indicative, I think.

Why actively monitor such statistics?

What methods are used?

How can a personal experience be categorized so broadly?

Do they feel changed?

Feelings can change, but have they –themselves– changed?

Are we actively changing in times or tenses as we minister?

A challenge it is to measure the metaphysical or spiritual in temporal terms.

Interact Here

Whose responsibility
is measurement?

Then what must one do to save as
well as be saved?

What was our LORD's
answer?

**Do we repent in increments;
is that best these days?**

Cultures and contexts change, but
what about the minds and the souls?

To the individual,
what does the SPIRIT say?

History has proven more effective
means with the multitudes.

**The πνέυμα blows where it
will.**

The seeds are
scattered, and —alas—
they land in diversity.

Variable: Salvation

1. Luke 13
2. Mark 10
3. Romans
4. Ephesians
5. 1 Corinthians
6. Galatians
7. Titus
8. Luke 8

Interact Here

Interact Here

Variable: Μαρτυρέω

How do we talk about our situation?

There are many beginnings.

'Tis a long story; most are aware of parts only.

How does one know which gaps need to be filled?

Somewhere along the way, the fractions became viewed as wholes.

What about those who have never known any?

Most have known hearsay.

Many others have been hurt.

Hallelujah.

Variable: Μαρτυρέω

1. Matthew 11
2. Revelation 2-3
3. Job 13
4. 1 Thessalonians

Interact Here

Interact Here

Variable: Prayer

What do you pray?

My prayers vary being sometimes much sometimes little in number; subject matter and frequency does vary as well.

There are times when others ask me to intercede on their behalf.

To what end?

Alas for the sanctified; they receive honor instead of pity, respect instead of company.

Glory to the Counselor, first; and it is such a versatile discipline.

Indeed, HE does record them according to HIS weights and standards.

I admit my means fall short of my ideals, but I am determined.

We all do; that discrepancy is covered and by faith made acceptable.

Not HIS role do I question but mine. If faith be requisite and HE is omniscient, then what is speech and thought?

Either way, I approach boldly.

That we should ramble as a heathen?

He knows the heart and soul; is that enough?

The residence of which is where and where words originate —which HE knows beforehand?

What is faith without expression?

What is faith without love?

What is faith without faith?

Interact Here

Interact Here | **Variable: Prayer**

1. Matthew 6
2. 1-2 Timothy 2
3. Romans 8
4. Ephesians 2
5. 1 Corinthians 13
6. James
7. 1 Thessalonians
8. John 3
9. Hebrews 4

Variable: Mystery

To what extent do you believe that faith has power?

What is beyond admission that treads not with folly?

To love with mind, heart, and soul -to know, feel, and be?

'Tis challenging to find them and establish equilibrium let alone to master.

The preceding mysteries displayed seem more detached of late.

That used to play such a role. What happened?

Sight is ludicrous to one who knows it not.

Admitting the unknown appears like weakness sometimes.

Interact Here

A mystery is mysterious by definition.

What of a symbol?

Faith in or faith shown by?

Other options are hidden, perhaps.

Certain rites, prayers, symbols, and Scriptures are known to resonate with individuals on some level -heart, soul, mind, or a combination.

If the faith of a pagan can summon demons and cast spells, then what are we doing with ours?

Angels and demons, witchcraft and magic, and tongues and prophecy: I do not have experience with these.

How and where should we tread?

Fear no evil ye
baptized with water and
fire.

Who wants to learn such things;
they are not elementary?

Without knowing faith,
how would you wield it?

Interact Here

Variable: Mystery

1. Matthew 3, 13
2. Ecclesiastes
3. Deuteronomy 6
4. Job 11
5. 2 Corinthians 11
6. Hebrews 13
7. Jude
8. Grandma Puscas

Variable: Claim

I observe when youths finish school, go to college, leave their parents, and meet the age requirements for adulthood and legal self-choice that few return to their faith, to the congregations of their youth.

There are a plethora of causes and effects regarding this.

Do we foster an environment where youths feel they can profess such faiths as their own?

Is there something for which to look forward; is adult faith appealing?

What a divide.

Truly, how much can we foster; are we ministering or are we sitting?

There must be some way, some method to anchor faith more effectively?

If such a tool were available, the goal you propose would require a paradigm shift, would it not?

Change is always resisted.

Losses can not be cut recklessly, but we can not dwell either.

I can not help that my mind does drift to the youths' homes and parents; their influence can not be overestimated.

Rebellion is inherent in development so long as success is questionable. Why do we not anticipate appropriately?

What of hooks?

Most see through lures and will grow to resent baubles as traps.

Interact Here

Interact Here

Some just need more convincing.

Who buys and sells?

Should we seek to give answers unasked, or should we seek to answer questions?

I have a tough time selling that which sells itself.

If it sold itself so well, then would not more youth return by choice?

Perhaps there is a disconnect?

How much faith is needed to believe, to receive grace when a seed moves mountains?

From whence does faith originate?

Indeed the source is, and He calls His.

What is it that we do?

I feel small.

Variable: Claim	Interact Here

1. Smith, Christian with Melinda Denton Lundquist. *Soul Searching: The Religious and Spiritual Lives of American Teenagers.* Oxford, NY: Oxford University Press, 2005.
2. Mark Twain

Variable: Integrate

With what do you have trouble regarding adult relationships and support?

One cannot lead those who wish it not.

Recruitment varies.

Why is this so?

The views of ministerial horizons differ between denominations, generations, expectations, and individuals.

Are we not one also? The hand is not a foot, yet both are attached to the whole.

What is it the laity desires? What of the clergy?

What would happen if there were no clergy but Scripture and Spirit only to influence thus?

Indeed, there are loins to gird, yet few are invested.

What can be done?

How might the paradigm be affected by de-compartmentalizing?

'Tis natural to defend though it may not behoove.

Can a parent drastically alter parenting styles halfway through a child's development without consequences?

Communication must be factored and overcome at the onset.

When every seed is nurtured, no good branch is pruned; when every branch is pruned, no seed is produced.

Woe that we have come to this. There must be a solution.

If interests were raised, could we –would we?

Interact Here

The efficiency ratio is a daunting hurdle.

If energy has a flow, then it can be altered.

Solitude is chosen; yet, some struggle alone.

Can we continue thusly?

"Do this in remembrance."

Variable: Integrate

1. Sun Tzu
2. Burns, Jim and Mike DeVries. *Partnering with Parents in Youth Ministry.* Gospel Light, 2003.
3. Ephesians 6
4. Job 38
5. Luke 12, 22
6. Chaos Theory
7. John 15
8. Acts 2
9. 1 Corinthians 11, 12

Variable: Rites

How are we taken as ministers by the whole?

Perhaps it is merely misinformation? The boundaries of ministry flow to and fro.

What is broadcast?

How are the youth seen by the rest?

Equality is rarely given; earned as with the discipline to exercise that equality.

What qualifications must be met in order to be a youth and then transition?

How is passage made acceptable?

If youthfulness is a given, then it can be utilized.

Without direction, the endorsement is destructive.

Should succession be?

It takes a tribe, sometimes.

How did it come to this?

Variable: Rites

1. Schults, Thom and Joani. *Why Nobody Learns Much of Anything at Church: and How to Fix It.* Loveland, CO: Group, 1993.
2. Mueller, Walt. *Youth Culture 101.* El Cajon, CA: Youth Specialties, 2007.

3. Black, Wesley, Chap Clark, Malan Nel, and Mark H. Senter III. *Four Views of Youth Ministry and the Church.* Grand Rapids, MI: Zondervan Publishing House, 2001.
4. Chromey, Rick. *Youth Ministry in Small Churches.* Loveland, CO: Group, 1990.
5. Chrichton, Michael. *Jurassic Park.* New York: Ballantine Books, 1990.

Interact Here

Variable: Recycle

How long have you been a minister of youth?

I have experience and of being replaced.

Transitions are often difficult.

Recovery is often long.

And every time, we must prove ourselves lest the ministry be in jeopardy.

Can this be made advantageous?

Breaking a cycle may lead to new ones with newer – unforeseen and, perhaps, more strenuous– consequences.

Instead of breaking, why not release or remake?

Do you think *use* and *expect* are more sound?

How did our predecessors experience this?

What did the successful ones prepare?

Those with hindsight are called wise; those with foresight are called prophet or disposable.

Preventing stagnation will prevent expiration, will it not?

Stirs benefit at the right times.

Should we set our feet to tarry or to wander?

How did the Apostles carry on?

Can those acts be reapplied?

Can the SPIRIT renew such context so far removed?

What will happen to our ministries once we are removed?

Interact Here

Interact Here

Do we plan our ministries to be dependent upon our involvement?

Variable: Recycle

1. Acts
2. Isaiah
3. Yoido Full Gospel Church, Seoul Korea

Variable: Many Mind

There are many demands for my attention.

Does the cup run over when the plate is full?

On what do you allow your mind to focus?

What is your discernment process?

Alas: wisdom and folly clutter.

A circumstantial response is standard.

Of doctrines and practices: what is primary, secondary, tertiary?

Do the parts come from or become the whole?

How can the distractions be utilized?

Interact Here

What of consistency?

What of vanity?

A time and a place: how can the peripheral benefit or dilute?

Compared to the central: is all without blemish or is blemish all we know?

Steady the mind may be; yet, my heart still beats.

Who are we to prune, then, if we feel not the cut?

'Tis felt. 'Tis always felt.

Naturally, the body desires equilibrium.

Alas, the mind is as weak as the flesh –so weak.

When chaos comes to cloud, how can I then find myself?

There are warnings.

Attention!

It is uphill and against the flow
but such is the place for' to go.

Uncomfortable: we all
encounter and then adjust
—lately— a generation too
late.

Interact Here

Variable: Many Mind

1. *The Last Samurai.*
   Movie: Warner
   Brothers, 2003.
2. Ecclesiastes
3. Romans

Variable: Passion

Where is Christ in our busy-ness?

On occasion, he seems to hide.

Of this, we sometimes use a language of fire.

Fire is fickle; for a flame in flux has life but finds itself finite.

How is it lost?

Some steadily seek to rekindle sparks in scheduled seclusions.

Behoove they may; yet events will end eventually.

Fleeting moments are infrequent; the rock endures.

The penitent shall pass.

How can this be taught? There are so few masters.

Ten percent is both big and small.

Youth is wasted on the young.

Effort weighs more when you procrastinate.

Prithee, focus.

Variable: Passion

1. Mike Yaconelli.
2. J.R.R. Tolkein
3. *V for Vendetta.* Movie: Warner Brothers, 2005.
4. Matthew 7
5. *Indiana Jones: The Last Crusade.* Movie: Lucasfilm Ltd., 1989.
6. *Bulletproof Monk.* Movie: Metro-Goldwyn-Mayer, 2003.
7. Luke 11

Interact Here

Variable: Ingenuity

How do you seek new talent, new ideas?

For what purpose?

Who would choose standing water over flowing?

Usually, I do not; though, need sometimes drives me: a volunteer or student will move on and leave a void.

Too many unexpected changes may affect.

Should we just wait for the potential to convert into the kinetic of their own accord?

To plan or to react, that is the question; 'tis arduous to find as well as refine.

Sometimes raw is more beneficial.

Have you ever taught
someone to drive?
Sometimes, I fear to
relinquish control.

Interact Here

Should you not?

Where is effort best spent?

If we find a system that works,
then why should we falter from it?

What works for one
may not to work for the
next but cycles past the
many, and the previous
may testify for this.

For what should we seek this?

When the purpose is my own, I find I am often devoid.

To seek and to guide or to arm
and unleash; both are reckless.

Perfection, where are
you?

The wise add sadness.

Interact Here	Variable: Ingenuity
	1. Ecclesiastes 1
	2. Joshua
	3. 1–2 Kings

Variable: Teach

What is the best way to teach?

That may depend upon the pupil's resonance with the teacher and the teaching.

That may depend upon the teacher's strengths and weaknesses.

Alas, that we cannot foresee hindsight.

For whom is experience the best lesson from which to learn?

How does one teach an infant to hear?

A manager can manage, and a coach can coach; but who can teach?

Who learns most from teaching?

For what is a student designed that a teacher should find difficulty?

Verily, space to spread one's wings is necessary, but I worry.

Fret not; failure behooves.

Perhaps roles could be tweaked and used as litmus?

Use caution: evaluation benefits but may prioritize the mind over the heart. Do we seek one over the other?

Quandary is not in the Material, the Text.

What of the means and forebears?

What does the SPIRIT say?

How did CHRIST teach his compared to us?

Variable: Teach

1. Icarus
2. All of CHRIST's
   parables

Interact Here

3. *Avatar: the Last Airbender.* TV Series: Nickelodeon, 2005–8.
4. Stevens, Jeanne. *"The Lost Art of Teaching through Story."* Youth Specialties, lecture. Nashville, TN, November 2005.
5. Lawrence, Rick ed. *Youth Ministry in the 21st Century.* Loveland, CO: Group, 2006.
6. Elwell, Walter A. and Robert W. Yarbrough. *Encountering the New Testament: a Historical and Theological Survey.* 2nd ed. Grand Rapids, MI: Baker Academic, 2005.

Variable: Disciple

We are ministers of youth, but just what is a "youth?"

We have used words like "teenagers" in times past, but the developing definition of our ministry expands our terms.

In times past, there were no teenagers. A child would become a man or a woman at the time of puberty and an adult at the time of marriage.

The classifications of the age groups expand –everyone must be unique and unified.

If it is expected to change, then it may be anticipated: who should be exempt?

Should we belittle past word choices? Carefully selected, language can annunciate truth and communicate mindset.

Walk, run, crawl?

These are some: those who are forced to come, those who attend bodily, those who attend cognitively, and those who seek the narrow.

'Tis more natural to seek the path of least resistance.

Who is to provide either?

Few seek difficulty let alone choose it once found; discipline and discipleship are hard to sell.

There are so many aspects.

Most examples can only be found in books, sadly. Interactions yield well.

How, then, may one proceed and succeed?

Who would choose adversity advertised at the onset?

Interact Here

Interact Here

Who are we not to advertise?

Is it a trap? Should we bait? Or do we wait for the few whilst babysitting the rest?

'Tis a choice, and the choice is theirs; yet so few choose.

Variable: Disciple

1. Foster, Richard J. *Celebration of Discipline: the Path to Spiritual Growth*. rev. ed. Harper SanFransisco, 1998.
2. Jones, Tony. *The Sacred Way: Spiritual Practices for Everyday Life*. Grand Rapids, MI: Zondervan, 2005.

3. King, Mike. *Presence-Centered Youth Ministry*. Downers Grove, IL: IVP Books, 2006.
4. Matthew, Mark, Luke, John, and Acts
5. Observe the cultural differences of adulthood and youth —i.e. Russian, Jewish, Greek, America, Korean

Interact Here

Interact Here

Variable: Danger

Physical persecution has not happened out in the open in our region in a very long time.

How could we have prepared?

Reliance on the Spirit outweighs; yet our loitering benefitted not.

What of tribulation benefits ministry?

Suffering with Christ differs from hard times to good.

For what is youth tamed?

Death comes to all.

Was not this place supposed to be different?

Our history is diverse. Often, we reconcile by honoring certain ones.

Negativity.

Of the hardened, fire
tested faith of our
forbears, are we capable?

What then, should we test?

Who would design and proctor?

There are challenges
when building on rock or
sand.

Must the seed be scattered?

Often I wonder, "What of the bad
soils?"

Who wants to know
the path is narrow and
troublesome —even for
the faithful?

Courage. Courage for our friends and for the choice.

Interact Here

Variable: Danger

1. C.S. Lewis
2. Matthew 7, 10, 11

65

Interact Here

3. Galatians
4. Acts
5. 2 Corinthians
6. Thomas, Dylan. *The Poems of Dylan Thomas*. "Do Not Go Gently Into That Good Night." Poem. New Directions Publishing Corporation, 1946.

Variable: Mission

Where did youth ministry come from; what was its original purpose?

Is it different now?

Mission statements are all slightly different.

Unique or un-unified, many parts or one body?

Are we succeeding?

Success is subjective.

As such, is it legitimate if we are serving ourselves not?

Failure is not an option either way.

How might standardization compliment or contradict denomination?

Interact Here

What is the endgame, and how many means lead thence?

The master plan of our scheming dictates —if such was done.

To be nearsighted or to be farsighted: that is the question.

Reliance on the Spirit is usually learned from the impulse of the Spirit.

We start and journey differently; there is one way to go, one race to run.

The enemy prepares.

So little did we know commencing.

Our undertaking seems daunting depending upon the vantage point.

How does youth ministry fit in the Church?

Can the disconnects be discerned?

Where are our eyes?

Whether content in their containment or not, indulgence deems desire.

Oh, do we see the same picture differently, or are we fixed upon many points?

Holistically, what are the most important aspects of the Church's ministry?

What are the least?

Quality or quantity; great or small?

Our LORD will know.

The temporal terms of reaction will be short and long.

Variable: Mission

1. 1 Corinthians 12

Interact Here

Interact Here

2. Five Iron Frenzy 2. *Electric Boogaloo.* CD. "Farsighted." Song: Five Minute Walk Records, 2001.

3. 1 John

4. Havergal, Frances Ridley. "*Take My Life.*" Hymn. 1847.

5. Lemmel, Helen H. "*Turn Your Eyes Upon Jesus.*" Hymn. 1922.

6. 1 &2 Timothy

Final Notes

I understand that the characters presented information in a difficult manner and few clues or answers are provided. Such is the nature of Dialogue. I propose a challenge to you regarding this: consider them.

Can you describe their characters after understanding their self-descriptions or after reading their words? What are the different ways in which they view ministry? Toward which emotion(s) does each one gravitate? Who are these Three? Are you more like one and more unlike another? How? Why? Of what avail would such similarities or dissimilarities have with you?

Character Challenge #1:

Canon Q. McKinsey

(formalis instabilitas; κανονικος κίνηση)

Character Challenge #2:

Filip Mann

(filius maneo; τέκνον χρόνιος)

Character Challenge #3:

Eudokia "Doc" Adams

(affectus adamans; ευδοκια άδαμας)

Additional Variables' Challenge

List and describe other variables of ministry that you have observed.

The Hypothesis Challenge

What is / are the hypotheses of the Youth Ministry experiment? Without applying a "good" or "bad" value to your hypotheses, have your hypotheses been proven or disproven thus far?

The Control Challenge

What is the control –or control group– of the Youth Ministry experiment?

Material, Subjects, and People Worth Referencing

1. The Holy Bible
2. Francis of Assisi, St.
3. Antony of Egypt, St.
4. Theresa of Avila, St.
5. John of the Cross, St.
6. Heraclitus
7. SØren Kiërkegaard
8. Apostle Paul, The
9. Galli, Mark. *131 Christians Everyone Should Know.* Nashville, TN: Broadman & Holman Publishers, 2000.
10. Greek and Latin
11. Cogdill, James. *Heart of Steel.* Baltimore, MD: Publish America, 2005.
12. John Donne

13. Oestriker, Mark & Mike Yaconelli.
    *What I wish I knew When I
    Started Youth Ministry: Stupid
    Misconceptions, and Caring
    for Your Own Soul While
    Ministering to Others.* El Cajon,
    CA: Youth Specialties, 2005.